The Unexplained

UFOs

by Terri Sievert

KANELAND MIDDLE SCHOOL
1N137 MEREDITH ROAD
MAPLE PARK, ILLINOIS 60151

Consultant:
Jerome Clark, Co-editor
International UFO Reporter
J. Allen Hynek Center for UFO Studies
Chicago, Illinois

Capstone
press

Mankato, Minnesota

Edge Books are published by Capstone Press
151 Good Counsel Drive, P.O. Box 669, Mankato, Minnesota 56002
www.capstonepress.com

Library of Congress Cataloging-in-Publication Data
Sievert, Terri.
    UFOs / by Terri Sievert.
    p. cm.—(Edge books. The unexplained)
    Includes bibliographical references and index.
    ISBN 0-7368-2714-5 (hardcover)
    1. Unidentified flying objects—Juvenile literature. [1. Unidentified flying objects.]
I. Title. II. Series.
TL789.2.S54 2005
001.942—dc22   2003026406

Summary: Describes the history, sightings, and possible causes of UFOs.

Editorial Credits
Angela Kaelberer, editor; Juliette Peters, designer; Kelly Garvin, photo researcher;
    Eric Kudalis, product planning editor

Photo Credits
Corbis/Bettmann, 15
Fortean Picture Library, 6, 11, 12, 17, 19, 20, 23, 25, 27, 28, 29; Dennis Stacy, 9;
    Klaus Arsleff, 5
Rubberball Productions, cover (background)

Artistic Effects
Capstone Press/Scott Thoms, cover (foreground)

1 2 3 4 5 6 09 08 07 06 05 04

Table of Contents

FEATURES

Chapter 1

A Crash in Roswell

On July 4, 1947, James Ragsdale was camping about 40 miles (64 kilometers) north of Roswell, New Mexico. Ragsdale saw a bright object fly overhead. It crashed to the ground about 1 mile (1.6 kilometers) from his campsite.

Ragsdale and a friend went to the crash site the next morning. They saw pieces of an aircraft. It had narrow wings and was shaped like a bat. The aircraft's front was buried in the ground.

Ragsdale said he also saw alien bodies. They were 4 to 5 feet (1.2 to 1.5 meters) tall. Ragsdale and his friend left the site when they saw military vehicles arriving.

Learn about:
- Roswell crash
- Alien bodies
- The military's role

A sign marks the place where a mysterious object crashed near Roswell in 1947.

Other Witnesses

Other people said they saw the alien bodies. Frank Kaufmann worked at Roswell Army Air Field. He said he visited the crash site with eight other men. Kaufmann said five bodies were inside the aircraft. The bodies had large heads and large eyes. Kaufmann said

▲ U.S. Army Air Force officials said the Roswell wreckage was part of a weather balloon.

the bodies were taken to a hospital at a military base.

Roswell funeral director Glenn Dennis said base officials called him. They asked about small caskets. Dennis said he later talked to a nurse from the base hospital. She told him the aliens had four fingers, no hair, and white skin.

The Rancher's Story

Rancher Mac Brazel also heard a crash in the area. Early the next morning, he found metallic scraps in his field. The lightweight material could not be cut or burned.

Brazel told a local sheriff what he had found. Members of the U.S. Army Air Force picked up the scraps. They told newspapers the scraps were from a flying disk. The next day, air force officials changed their story. They said the wreckage was part of a weather balloon.

Questions

Many experts doubt the people who say they saw aliens at Roswell. At first, James Ragsdale said he saw four alien bodies. He later said he saw nine bodies. He claimed he buried them in the sand. The stories of Frank Kaufmann and Glenn Dennis also have been questioned.

Other people think the military is hiding the truth. These people believe the crashed aircraft was an alien spacecraft. They say the air force hid the alien bodies. The stories add to the mystery of unidentified flying objects, or UFOs.

⬆ Many people believe the alien bodies were stored in Hangar 84 at Roswell Army Air Field.

Chapter 2

History of UFOs

In the late 1940s, some people who reported UFOs described them as disk-shaped. People started calling them "flying saucers." Other UFO shapes have also been reported.

The U.S. Air Force groups UFOs into four types. They are flying disks, torpedo- or cigar-shaped objects, round or balloon-shaped objects, and balls of light.

Learn about:
• Types of UFOs
• Famous sightings
• Alien encounters

This flying disk was photographed in New Mexico in 1957.

Flying Disks

On June 24, 1947, Kenneth Arnold was flying an airplane over the state of Washington. He saw something strange in the sky. Nine silvery objects darted between Mount Rainier and Mount Adams. The object in front was shaped like a crescent. The others were shaped

▼ In 1947, Kenneth Arnold showed a drawing of one of the objects he saw near Mount Rainier.

like pie pans with triangles in the rear. Arnold later said they were traveling at least 1,200 miles (1,900 kilometers) per hour and were 50 feet (15 meters) long.

The objects Arnold saw were among the first UFOs. They have never been explained.

Sighting from the Sky

The night of October 18, 1973, was clear and dark. Four army reserve members flew in a helicopter over Mansfield, Ohio. The crew members saw a red light beaming in the distance. They then saw a flying object. It flew toward them so fast they thought it would hit the helicopter.

As the object came closer, crew members saw it was gray and shaped like a cigar. It had a dome on its top and a red light on its front. It had a green beam underneath and a white light on its back.

The crew's sighting lasted nearly 5 minutes. People on the ground also reported seeing the lights and object in the sky.

The object has never been explained. Some people think it was a new type of aircraft. Others think it was a meteor. Others doubt these explanations. The crew members saw the object for several minutes. An aircraft or meteor would not have stayed in sight of the crew for that amount of time.

A Red Moon

On September 3, 1965, several people spotted a round, red object in the night sky near Exeter, New Hampshire. One person said it looked like a red moon. It moved slowly through the air just above the trees.

The air force investigated the Exeter sighting. It found no explanation.

Balls of Light

Another unexplained sighting happened in Michigan in 1966. On March 21, 87 college students saw a large glowing object fly over a field in Hillsdale. The ball of light was shaped like a football. The night before, people in Dexter, Michigan, had seen a similar light over a swamp.

On October 4, 1967, people in Nova Scotia, Canada, saw an object flitting along the coast. One witness said it looked like an orange light following the shoreline. The object appeared to crash into the Atlantic Ocean near the town of Shag Harbour. The object was never explained.

▲ In March 1966, people in Michigan searched the night sky for balls of glowing light.

Aliens

Some UFO sightings go beyond seeing an object. Some people say they have met aliens from other planets. People also report being taken aboard alien spaceships.

On September 19, 1961, Betty and Barney Hill were driving on U.S. Highway 3 in New Hampshire. A bright light followed them. They stopped their car and looked at the object through binoculars. They said they saw a large spaceship with rows of windows. They continued driving and heard a beeping sound. Both of the Hills felt sleepy.

They suddenly realized they were 35 miles (56 kilometers) farther south. Two hours had passed. They did not know what had happened to them during that time.

The Hills were later hypnotized. They told of being examined by aliens. After their experience, the Hills said they had headaches and other health problems. In 1969, Barney Hill died after a blood vessel burst in his brain. Since 1961, Betty Hill has investigated UFO reports and has written about her experiences.

EDGE FACT

About 3 million people in the United States believe
they have had a close encounter with alien beings.

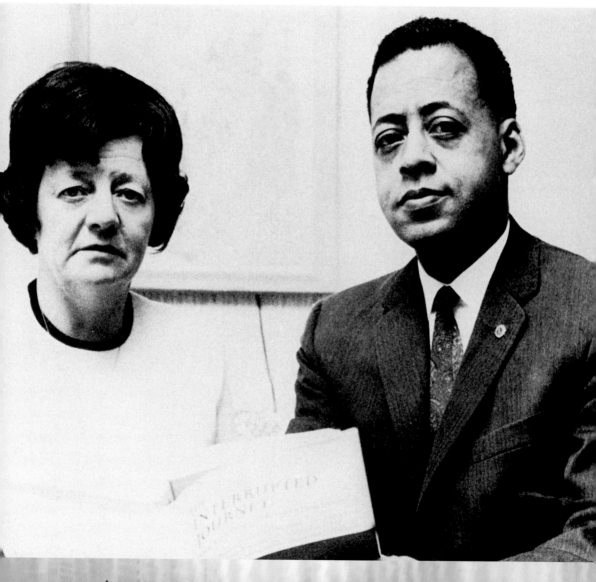

▲ Betty and Barney Hill said they were kidnapped by aliens.

Chapter 3

UFO Hunters

In 1948, the U.S. Air Force first used the term "unidentified flying object." The term described an airborne object that could not be explained. Between 1948 and 1969, the air force studied unusual objects sighted in the sky. The air force decided that UFOs were either natural objects or hoaxes. But many people do not accept that explanation.

Edward Condon

In the 1960s, University of Colorado professor Edward Condon became interested in UFOs. He and his staff talked to people who had seen UFOs. They also looked for scientific evidence.

Learn about:
- Air force studies
- Condon report
- J. Allen Hynek

Air force workers called
one of their UFO studies
Project Blue Book.

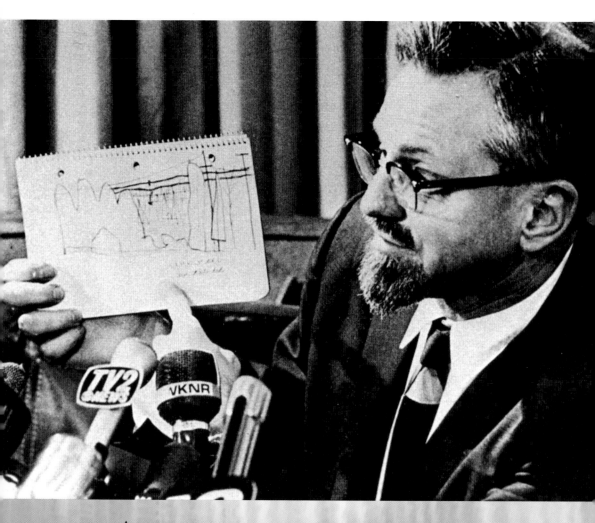

In 1966, J. Allen Hynek spoke to reporters about the balls of light sighted in Michigan.

Condon believed UFO spotters saw something they could not explain. He described UFOs as objects in the sky that have an unknown origin. But he did not find evidence that UFOs are spacecraft from other planets.

Other Researchers

Astronomer J. Allen Hynek studied UFO sightings for the U.S. Air Force from the 1940s until the 1960s. He interviewed people who claimed to have seen UFOs. He developed a system to classify the different types of UFO sightings. In 1973, Hynek founded the Center for UFO Studies (CUFOS) near Chicago. He was its director until he died in 1986.

Other researchers continue Hynek's work. CUFOS member Jennie Zeidman is known for her report on the 1973 sighting by the helicopter crew in Ohio. Karl Pflock began investigating UFOs in the late 1960s. At the time, Pflock worked for the Central Intelligence Agency (CIA). Writer Budd Hopkins says he first saw a UFO in 1964. Since then, he has investigated about 700 UFO sightings.

UFO Sighting Classification System

Distant sightings—more than 500 feet (152 meters) away

Nocturnal lights—lights in the night sky that cannot be explained by known sources; these lights are often red, blue, orange, or white

Daylight disks—oval- or disk-shaped objects seen in the daytime

Radar-visual cases—unidentified signals that appear on radar screens at the same time and place as visual sightings of UFOs

Close sightings—within 500 feet (152 meters)

Close encounter of the first kind—a sighting of a UFO that does not interact with people or the environment

Close encounter of the second kind—a UFO sighting that has some effect on the environment, such as burned ground or trees

Close encounter of the third kind—a sighting of an alien being

▲ Some UFOs are spotted during the day, like this one
photographed near Albuquerque, New Mexico, in 1963.

Chapter 4

The UFO Question

Some objects reported as UFOs turn out to be identified flying objects (IFOs). Many IFOs are natural objects that people do not recognize.

Mistaken UFOs

Some IFOs are natural objects in the sky. Meteors, planets, and cloud formations are sometimes mistaken for UFOs.

People build other IFOs. New types of aircraft are sometimes mistaken for UFOs because people are not familiar with them. Weather balloons and searchlights also have been called UFOs.

Learn about:
- IFOs
- Hoaxes
- Unexplained sightings

Some cloud formations are mistaken for UFOs. These lenticular clouds look like flying disks.

Natural Explanations

Some UFO sightings are optical illusions. Sunlight reflecting off ice crystals or a bird's wings looks like a UFO to some people.

Mirages also are mistaken for UFOs. Reflecting rays of light at different air temperatures cause mirages. An object may appear to float in the sky.

Marsh gas can be mistaken for a UFO. Decaying swamp plants produce the glowing gas. Some people believe the 1966 sightings in Michigan were marsh gas.

Hoaxes

Since the 1800s, people have tried to make other people believe in UFO hoaxes. In 1896, an object crashed in a field near San Francisco. The object looked like an iron cone. It had wings and propellers. Two people stumbled out of the object. One person later admitted they used a wagon to pull the object to the top of a hill. They then pushed the object over the hill.

Photos of UFOs can be faked. One photo of a supposed UFO was really a drop of milk. The photo was taken with high-speed film just as the milk splashed on the floor.

EDGE FACT

Some people link crop circles to UFOs. The circles form when plants in part of a field are flattened in a circular pattern. Many UFO experts think the crop circles are made by wind or by people.

▼ The person who took this photo said the object was a UFO. It was really a button.

Sighting at Socorro

Some UFO sightings remain puzzling. One of these sightings happened April 24, 1964, near Socorro, New Mexico.

Police officer Lonnie Zamora saw a flame in the sky. It landed behind a hill.

Zamora drove toward the hill. He saw a smooth, shiny oval object. Two small figures were near the object. He then heard slams and a loud roar. The object zipped into the air. The figures had disappeared.

People still wonder what Zamora saw. Some people think the aircraft was a hoax. Others think it was a test spacecraft. But these explanations have not been proven.

Unsolved Mystery

People have many beliefs about UFOs. Some people fear

▼ In 1964, Lonnie Zamora chased a UFO.

that UFOs carry unfriendly beings from other planets. Others hope UFOs will bring information about life on other planets. Still others do not believe UFOs exist at all.

Scientists will continue to study UFO sightings. They hope to someday solve the mystery of the strange objects and lights in the sky.

▼ Zamora said the Socorro UFO left these marks in the dirt.

Glossary

alien (AY-lee-uhn)—a creature from another planet

astronomer (uh-STRON-uh-mur)—a scientist who studies stars, planets, and other objects in space

casket (KASS-kit)—a long, narrow box into which a dead person is placed for burial

crescent (KRESS-uhnt)—a curved shape that looks like the moon when it is a sliver in the sky

hoax (HOHKS)—a stunt that tricks people into believing something that is not true

hypnotize (HIP-nuh-tize)—to put another person in a sleeplike state

meteor (MEE-tee-ur)—a piece of rock or dust that enters the earth's atmosphere, causing a streak of light in the sky

mirage (muh-RAHZH)—a reflection of a distant object; mirages are caused by light rays bending where air layers of different temperatures meet.

Read More

Herbst, Judith. *UFOs.* The Unexplained. Minneapolis: Lerner, 2005.

Krull, Kathleen. *What Really Happened in Roswell?: Just the Facts (Plus the Rumors) about UFOs and Aliens.* New York: HarperCollins, 2003.

Mason, Paul. *Investigating UFOs.* Forensic Files. Chicago: Heinemann Library, 2003.

Internet Sites

FactHound offers a safe, fun way to find Internet sites related to this book. All of the sites on FactHound have been researched by our staff.

Here's how:
1. Visit *www.facthound.com*
2. Type in this special code **0736827145** for age-appropriate sites. Or enter a search word related to this book for a more general search.
3. Click on the **Fetch It** button.

FactHound will fetch the best sites for you!

Index